THE ART OF ATTRACTING WOMEN:

FINDING EXACTLY WHAT YOU WANT

BY

JONATHAN YARNOLD

R&E Publishers

R&E Publishers
P.O. Box 2008, Saratoga, CA 95070
Tel: (408) 866-6303   Fax: (408) 866-0825

Book Cover and Illustrations by Kaye Quinn
Typesetting by elletro Productions

ISBN 1-56875-041-2

L.C. 93-083491

Designed, typeset and totally manufactured in the United States of America.

DEDICATION

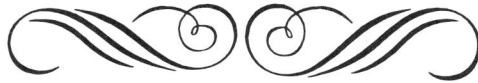

I dedicate this book to my wonderful wife, Alessandra. Since I have met her, my life has become full of meaning and excitement. It really is mind-blowing to me to think that two years ago I was cruising along without a care in the world and then out of coincidence, I met the most dynamic, passionate and caring woman that I could ever imagine. She has been the true driving force behind this project. Seemingly, every time I needed a little boost, she was there for me. I look forward to many projects together with her...my precious Alessandra.

ACKNOWLEDGMENTS

I would like to acknowledge the following people who have had a profound impact on this project as well as my life. I would first and foremost like to thank my parents, Stanley and Kay Yarnold. Obviously, without them I would not be here. They have provided an amazingly solid foundation for me—one that has allowed my creative juices to flow without restriction. One would think that most parents, especially fathers, tend to push their children in a more conservative direction than the one that I have taken. However, my mom and dad have acted quite the opposite. Whether it be an encouraging word over the phone, or a loving hug, they both have a unique quality about them that exudes confidence. I constantly have been encouraged to "go for it" by them, in whatever endeavor I have chosen. I love them both dearly.

My sister Deborah, who is, and always will be "Deb" to me, has also had an impact on me. When this book was in its infantile stage, I told her about it and she bubbled with excitement. "Keep at it, I just know it'll be great", she told me over and over. Now, with all of the scraps of paper with notes scribbled on them tucked away somewhere in my unbelievably messy closet, the book is completed. I want to thank her for her positive thoughts and our late night conversations...I won't ever forget them.

John Ghio is like a brother to me. We have been the closest of friends since we first played sandlot baseball together close to twenty years ago. He has had a lot of input into this project and I am very grateful to the hours upon hours we spent discussing various topics for the book. I would write drafts and Johnny and my wife would sit around and listen to me reading aloud. I appreciate him as would anyone who understands what is a "true" friend.

CONTENTS

LET'S
NOT
TAKE THIS
TOO SERIOUSLY

LET'S NOT TAKE THIS TOO SERIOUSLY

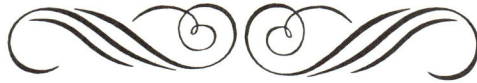

One thing that you need to understand about the content of this book is that I have tried to stay away from creating a drab textbook about a "serious interaction among the sexes". I have attempted to keep everything as simple as possible, even though there are some pretty tricky areas in the dating scene.

The key is to be aggressive, make mental notes of what works and what doesn't, and to keep going for it. Women are human and they are filled with insecurities like the rest of us. Therefore, the way you treat them is a very delicate matter when it comes to attracting them or driving them away. Our imaginations run wildly when dealing with the opposite sex, so it really is best to stay focused on what you want.

I have never tried to take the whole meeting and dating scene too seriously, because it isn't. Sure, we get our hearts broken from time to time, and things don't always work out as we had hoped, but you still can't get too caught up in it all.

How delicate of a matter are we talking about? Well, for example, if you're too serious, it could be a turn-off to some women. If you're not serious enough, this could also be a turn-off. What does this mean? It means that you have to have happy mediums...with everything.

Extremes are also turn-offs. For example, if you are always too accommodating, a woman could possibly lose interest. If you are constantly unmotivated towards certain areas, this can also turn a woman away. However, if you treat women with respect and passion, they will tend to overlook your faults. Or at least give you some time to improve on them.

How do you do this? Well, that is explained, simply, in the following chapters. Use everything to your best advantage or pick and choose from the information that is given. By the end of the book, I believe that you'll have a better grasp of what I am trying to say. You'll also have a clearer picture of what you need to change, if anything.

Remember, don't be too serious. Life really is too short. There are many other things to worry about than how complex women are, and all of the other facets that encompass them. They are the same as us, humans looking for companions to fulfill basic needs. Remind yourself of this throughout the book and for the rest of your life. It will keep things in perspective and more importantly, simple.

DECIDING
WHAT YOU
WANT

DECIDING
WHAT YOU WANT

Millions of beautiful, single women flock to bars every weekend. One strategy for males is to be aggressive, attempt to buy one of them a drink, get her drunk, and then try to have your way. This, in theory, is not a bad strategy if you are only trying to "get laid" that evening.

Another strategy is to lay low, occasionally make eye contact with a potential willing candidate, wait until she is drunk, and then pounce on her with every persuasive way known to mankind while she has no clue what is really going on.

I have witnessed both of these strategies night in and night out in the bar "scene". I have to admit that with the right combination of circumstances, you too can get "lucky" on occasion at your favorite club.

However, the great majority of men put too much stock into these strategies. Believe me, they are usually costly and ineffective.

You have to decide what you want in a woman. What type of woman are you attracted to? If it's a quality, worldly woman you are looking for, it's really going to be tough finding her in a bar. However, if you really just want to get laid, by any willing female, then I wish you luck in your pursuits. One thing to remember though, is that the aforementioned strategies only happen on rare occasions, and they usually leave most men shooting blanks at the end of an evening. You definitely need a fresh and effective approach, with new strategies.

If you sit back and think about it(I know that I have), every day the potential to attract a female is overwhelming. On the contrary, most of the time men really do believe that you have to be in a bar or nightclub to attract and meet someone. Right here and now, your attitude must change. I bartended for many years, and from personal experience I know that bars and nightclubs are two of the worst places to try to attract quality women.

It's very easy to believe that bars are great meeting grounds because of how these establishments are marketed. "Ladies Night" and "Singles Only Night" are two examples of mere marketing and advertising that clubs use to attract new customers, as well as regulars. "I generally don't have any luck, but maybe this time will be different" is the type of thinking that these bars prey upon.

Most nightclubs survive because of their high liquor profit, and horny, nervous men drink tons of liquor. The majority of these men who get really drunk every time out usually go home by themselves. This is the case just about every night.

Why? The reason is because quality females are pretty smart in detecting horny, over anxious men, and this is why they do not go to a bar to seriously try to meet anyone. Most of them just go to "hang out" with their girlfriends and people-watch.

So many times I have heard women say, "Geez this guy kept asking me to dance, and he kept sending over drinks the entire night...Then he asked for my phone number so that we could 'get together sometime'...There is no way I would ever give my number to a guy in a bar... that's so sleazy."

Despite the fact that men never really get anywhere in the bar scene, they keep coming back and spending more and more hard-earned cash, and getting hornier and lonelier in the process.

I have met some very beautiful and bright women in bars, but the stigma of "I met him in a bar...it will never work out" or "How can I tell people where I met him" hangs over the heads of many women.

It's almost as if women have immediate radar built within themselves when they enter a bar or nightclub. They know that men are "wolves", both horny and lonely, and looking for an easy score. A warning system apparently goes off inside of them and blares out, "Wolves incoming...Protect yourself, you're in a bar."

I am sure that there are some exceptions to these generalizations. Some women really do want to meet a nice guy, regardless of where they happen to meet him. However, these exceptions are too few and far between and the odds of meeting one of these women are pretty bad. You, as a male, want to increase your odds of attracting someone, not worsen them.

Even though you are probably not a "wolf" and you are a nice guy, previous "wolves" have created very believable stereotypes about themselves and their behavior in bars. They have, in actuality, ruined it for all of us.

If you really believe in bars and the myths attached to them, let me give you a few examples of why you shouldn't have too much faith in them.

Some Myths Concerning the Bar Scene:

(1)   Pick-up lines work. On occasion, if you come up with something exceptionally witty, a good line can get a conversation rolling. However, on the whole, lines generally sound too practiced and "cheesy". A woman can spot a line a mile away - so try and avoid using one.

(2)   Sending over a drink is a great way to meet a woman. Most women feel threatened by this gesture. Many say, "Why didn't he just come over and say 'Hello' if he wanted to meet me?" This is a very wimpy way of trying to meet someone. Women feel that they "have" to talk to a guy who sends over a drink to them, rather than "want" to talk. If you are already

engaged in a conversation with a woman, and the both of you are finished with your drinks, offering to buy her a drink is okay in this situation. It's both friendly and unthreatening as well. Never use this gesture as a means of "trying to pick her up."

(3)   By flashing a fancy watch or a wallet loaded with cash, you can buy a woman's attraction. Admittedly, some women are attracted to money, and the flashy tangibles it provides. But who really wants to attract because of this reason? If this is the type you want to attract, then go for it. But keep in mind that most quality women are going to be attracted to you, not your wallet.

BEING
HONEST WITH
YOURSELF

BEING HONEST WITH YOURSELF

From this point on, if you really want to become attractive, or more attractive to women, you have to be completely honest with yourself. This starts with taking a look in the mirror and honestly analyzing what you see.

Maybe you are the perfect physical specimen and you are absolutely gorgeous in the eyes of many women. Well, if this is the case, you do not need to proceed any further with this chapter. If you notice that maybe you are not so perfect- congratulate yourself because you are perfectly normal.

Remember that generally, unless you are already involved in a conversation, initial attraction from a woman comes from a physical point of view. Thus, you want to be as attractive as possible, physically.

Maybe you feel you are too tall, too short, too fat or too thin. There is nothing wrong with these feelings, as they are pretty common among everyone. But to dwell on them is a mere waste of time.

Fashion and style, covered in later chapters, can disguise many of one's physical shortcomings, so I wouldn't worry about them right now. What you do need to think about is what looks "funny" or unattractive to you.

Maybe your neck is too long, or your feet are too big. Whatever the case, stop worrying about these areas. Just take note of what you like and dislike and store it away. Try to always remember how these attributes make you feel, because once you are finished with this book, you won't have to worry about them any longer.

FOCUSING ON YOUR POSITIVE QUALITIES

FOCUSING ON YOUR POSITIVE QUALITIES

Throughout this book, it's mentioned that you should be honest with yourself. When doing this, and while evaluating yourself at the same time, you should try to discover some of your most positive qualities.

You'll find that if you do this, not only will you feel your self-esteem rising- but those around you will feel the positive effects as well.

Here's an example of what I mean. I went to a comedy club in San Francisco once with a few friends- two of them being women. Before the show we were out in the lobby and this guy came over and started to talk briefly with one of the women. He had to leave about two minutes later, and we had to get to our seats. I kept kidding my woman friend and asking her if she liked the guy. She said that she had only talked to him for two minutes and that she didn't find him attractive in the least.

However, once the show started, we realized that the emcee was this very guy. He not only presented himself as hilarious, but bright and witty as well. After his set, I asked my friend what she thought of him at that point. "He's cute", she replied. When I asked her whether she would go out with him, she responded with a very definite "Sure I would...he seems like a great guy". Keep in mind that this comedian was not the model-type in any way, shape or form. My friend generally dated physically attractive business men. These men dressed well and were well educated. Yet, for some reason she found this very average looking guy attractive.

This comedian obviously had humor as one of his

positive and attractive qualities. He realized this and probably became a comedian because of this realization.

The point is that you should do the same and focus on your positive qualities. Concentrating on the negative ones will get you nowhere, and you'll be a virtual "drag" to be around.

Personality is so important in everyday life especially when it comes to attracting a woman. Many times a woman will find a guy absolutely gorgeous physically, yet when they talk to him they don't find him attractive any more. Why? Because this person probably didn't have much of a personality.

You need to let the real "you" come out and let your personality flow. If you are funny, go with it. If you find that you are a good listener, go with it. Do whatever you feel you are best at, and work on the areas that you aren't. Allow yourself the privilege of becoming comfortable with "you", and others will become more than comfortable being around you.

CONFIDENCE

CONFIDENCE

Confidence is one of the biggest attraction factors known. Why? The reason is because there are certain distinct qualities that make people want to be around those who have, or project the image of having, confidence.

Confidence connotes comfort, a sense of well-being, strength and positivity. Women are greatly attracted to all of these factors. Just as in the case when a confident man walks into a room—people notice...especially women.

Take a little test with yourself. Do you think a woman wants to be around someone who is constantly worrying about things?Do you think any woman wants to be around someone who is weak? (willed, not necessarily strength) How about being around someone who is constantly negative—do you find this quality attractive? Hopefully your answer is "no" to all of these questions.

Many times, men get intimidated by other men whom they perceive as confident. This is probably due to the fact that our insecurities prey on situations like these. The first response is, "That guy is such a jerk...he's so lucky".

On the contrary, women want to get closer to men who are sure of themselves and seem to know "where they are going." Why? Because they are attracted to that positivity.

You may be saying, "I'm confident...so why don't women flock to me like I want them to?" Well, you may be totally confident in your abilities, but somehow, the message is not coming across loud enough, or clear enough to others.

Here are some basic guidelines to projecting one's confidence:

(1) **STAND UP STRAIGHT.** Someone who slouches seems weak and unconfident. By standing up straight you project both poise and strength.

(2) **KEEP SMILING**. If you are standing up straight and you have a pleasant look of being comfortable on your face-you will naturally project confidence. What type of smile you use is a different story. For example, you shouldn't use the type of Cheshire-cat smile that women perceive as phony or sleazy. Rather, use one that is natural and looks as though you are having a good time.

Many times I have heard women, when asked why they were initially attracted to someone, reply "I don't know really...but he had a nice smile and seemed like a fun guy". Remember, there are distinctly some profound differences from being obnoxious and cocky and being confident.

Winning a woman's affection doesn't come from being louder than the next guy or bragging loudly about how much money you make. No one likes to be around obnoxious jerks. Yes, when they walk into a room, they get noticed...but for the wrong reasons. They are the ones that women want to avoid, not meet.

Maybe you are the nervous, anxiety-ridden type. You need to come to the realization that the sooner you start practicing and projecting confidence, the easier it will be for you every day. It's pretty typical for men to be nervous around the opposite sex, but women never have to know this.

Nervousness is not very attractive. So from this point on, let's work on disguising and ridding ourselves of it. All it takes is a little practice. After all, women are just human beings like you and me, so let's reduce our thinking to this state and keep it there.

It's easy to be comfortable with any situation once you are comfortable with yourself. You can't worry about the extra weight you have around you for now. Don't worry about how skinny certain clothes make you look. Get comfortable with yourself now and make the most of now. In most cases, worrying and having a self-defeatist attitude is a waste of energy.

If you are uncomfortable with something about you- change it. Make the extra effort to change, continue doing so and stay positive. Self-pity should have no place in your life. If you worry that you don't look as good as you possibly could- you'll get nowhere. Positivity is confidence. Believe in this and you'll be immensely happier in the long run. So will the women you meet!

RUTS

RUTS

Most men are great at coming up with excuses for why they don't meet any quality women. "All the good ones have boyfriends", they say, or, "They only go for the assholes—you know, the ones with all of the money and cars." One of my favorites is "The fine ones are all stuck up. They have so much attitude you can't even get near them."

In reality, the reason most men do not meet many women is because they are in a rut. What is a rut? To explain it is to probably describe many people's daily lifestyles.

Most of the time, people go to work, go home, eat dinner and go to sleep. The weekend comes at the end of a long workweek and maybe they'll head to a favorite bar or nightclub. They have a few belts (i.e. drinks) and attempt, usually unsuccessfully, to meet new members of the opposite sex. They then head home and Monday beckons. It's then back to the old routine again. Sound familiar? Many respond to this question by answering with something such as "Well, yeah, that is pretty much my routine, but I don't have time for anything else."

Weak...Weak...Weak excuse. All excuses are just that...weak. You just cannot expect the perfect woman to knock on your door and say, "Hi, I'm bright and gorgeous and very willing to go out with you."

C'mon, let's get back to reality. This probably will never happen and you probably know that it won't.

So many people I have met don't even know that they're in ruts, let alone know what one is. That is really what this is all about. You are in a rut, but you don't realize it. Life is basic, you do basically the same things all of the time, and you're fairly happy...you guess.

You must create change in your life to break out of a rut! A lot of my friends complain of "slumps", and maybe you and your friends complain of them as well. Slumps are extended periods of time when you don't meet any women. You need to realize at this point that slumps are mythical and nothing more than mere excuses.

You just simply cannot do the same things over and over and expect to attract someone of the opposite sex without some creativity on your part. If you start mixing up your interests, and you begin altering your circles and patterns of daily lifestyle and activities, you will be doing yourself a huge favor.

"How do I do this?" you ask. Actually, it's easier than you think. If you normally shop at a certain store at a certain time, you need to mix up the time, the store, or both. If you only work out at certain times because of your work schedule, consider switching gyms. Start hiking on the weekends or develop new hobbies, especially ones geared toward group events, such as biking. The key is to alter your normal patterns in order to increase your odds of meeting new women.

Convenience is such a large part of the reason why we do certain things at set times. Convenience stores, for example, are open twenty-four hours a day, allowing us to shop when it's convenient for us. You need to make the extra effort to change your patterns and to not always do the things that are easiest and most convenient. Remember that sometimes, actions that seemingly have to be done at certain times can be changed, and we can easily adapt to these changes.

If you find yourself complaining, catch yourself and get out of your rut. If you are constantly changing your lifestyle, not only will your chances of attracting and meeting women increase, but you will find yourself growing individually as well.

There are so many different types of wonderful women out there, and you need to put yourself in environments where they happen to be. If you change things at first and still do not find any attractive women, keep changing things. It's the only way to avoid ruts. They are life killers, and you must avoid them like the plague.

ATTITUDE

ATTITUDE

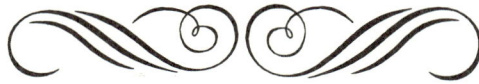

If the world in your eyes is just not happening in the female department, it is time for a drastic change in attitude. Attitude is so very important if you want to attract quality women in the 90's. The reason for this is because people, especially women, can detect the type of attitude you have even if they don't talk to you. It is displayed in your posture, mannerisms and by your facial expressions.

The attitude that you need to have if you want to be attractive to women is one that exudes confidence. You also must be ready and willing to attract at any given moment.

It all begins when you wake up in the morning. Sound ridiculous? Not when it comes to preparing yourself properly for meeting the quality woman of your dreams. You must begin focusing on the correct state of mind to attract. How do you do this? Start by looking in the mirror. Look at your positive qualities, and try to forget the negatives. You must pump yourself up, because no one else is going to. If you have really skinny legs, wear pants to cover them up. If you have too much around the middle, wear a baggy shirt to hide the fat. Start feeling as attractive as possible and start believing that anything really is possible...because it is.

I have always assumed the right attitude by firing myself up as soon as I wake up, thinking about the great possibilities of meeting someone. To get the phone number of, or to set up a date with, a new, exciting woman is all the inspiration I have ever needed. Before I started lifting weights, I was as skinny as a rail. I never let this discourage me though. I knew that women like nice, fun guys, and that I was one of those guys. Nothing is impossible, I thought, with the right attitude. So, instead of looking at how skinny I was, I looked at my smile and said that I could get any woman with it. "You're pretty funny...and you're not so bad looking...you've got nothing to lose" I would tell myself. Then I would go out and meet women I never before dreamed that I could.

I would be happier, more optimistic, and really excited about all of the possibilities of adventurous encounters. It became like a game. This way, I never took it too seriously, and I never got down on myself due to rejection.

Maybe this sounds too unbelievable, but it really does work. Just take a look at the opposite way of thinking. if you start your day off worrying about your job, or how you need to work out more, or how you lack women in your life, odds are that you'll be pretty down for most of the day. Unbeknownst to you, you probably also blow a lot of opportunities to meet women throughout the day- if your work environment is one that provides the possibilities. If all you do is take a self-pitying, "woe is me" attitude about meeting women, you'll never get anywhere.

However, if you start off focusing on being more positive, you'll eventually be positive...every day, all day. You must take the attitude of "I can't wait to get out there...I never know who I am going to meet."

You have to believe that in any given situation, at anytime, and in any place, the potential to attract and meet a female is there. The reason you must believe this is because it really is true!

I have always looked for the opportunity to meet someone, and this behavior has paid off greatly. There have been countless times when I would go out for just an hour or so, running errands, and I would come back home with a phone number or a date for later in the week. I have shaken my head many times, thinking that my luck was exceptional.

But when I compared my attitude with those of my friends' attitudes, who weren't as "lucky" as me, I realized that I was more confident, more aggressive, and more friendly as well. If you take the same type of initiative, you too can have "exceptional luck".

So many people,(especially those who happen to be married...not to scare you off) when asked where they had met their mates begin with, "That is such a funny story..." The places where people meet(see chapter on Where You Can Meet 'Em) are very unique as well as very routine. The difference between the two is the attitude people take towards their lives.

The supermarket might be very boring and routine to you, but to someone else, it's a social experience to go shopping for groceries. The reason for this is because of the way someone views a certain situation- whether it be in a negative or a positive manner. You must view the idea of meeting new women in a very positive way. It's the only real way any of this works. With the wrong attitude, you'll find yourself getting nowhere in a hurry.

You can't take this too seriously, because women get turned off if you are too businesslike in your pursuits. This is fun and it makes life unpredictable and exciting. Allow it to be this way or you'll make yourself miserable by creating a science out of it all.

Right now, there are literally millions of single women out there. "Where?", you ask. Well, everywhere you look, really. For starters, you must open up your eyes and take the blinders off because these women are out there. If you look deeper than just cosmetics, there are many bright, dynamic and beautiful females around, you just need to find them. They're ready to meet someone like you and with the right attitude, you'll come across more women than you'll be able to handle. Stay positive, and start now!

BEING
ALERT AND
FRIENDLY

♥

BEING ALERT AND FRIENDLY

I have always believed in catching people's, especially women's, eyes and nodding, or saying "Hello". As a result of this practice, many conversations have ensued as well as many friendships.

I can count virtually hundreds of times when I have met women this way. Just by being friendly, you can actually meet women without even saying some cheesy "line". Sounds too easy? Well, start believing because it really is as simple as it sounds.

Wherever I am, I follow this practice, and you should as well. Being friendly is disarming and unthreatening to people, and it's too bad that most people act quite the opposite.

Here's a typical example of an instance that occurs daily. You are at a supermarket and you notice a very attractive woman in the same aisle. Most men will either lust after the woman and follow her around like puppies, or they'll glance at them, stare at them, get their hearts pounding, and run off with their tails between their legs.

A great, easy way to meet a woman in this situation is to first make eye contact with her in some way. If it means grabbing for the same item as her or accidentally getting into her way, do whatever you feel is best. Then, if the allows it, smile and say "Excuse me" and then "Hi"! You must remember that you have nothing to lose by saying "Hello"—to anyone for that matter.

What really is the worst case scenario? Would it be that she doesn't respond at all? Or maybe she half-smiles and walks the other way? Whatever the response may be-

Who cares? You have nothing to lose and everything to gain.

Maybe only one out of every twenty women you say "Hello" to responds, and maybe you'll only make a date with one out of every twenty who respond. Whatever the numbers are, it seems like a pretty small percentage doesn't it? Well, if you don't say "Hello" or act friendly to anyone, what kind of response can you expect?

Zero...Zilch...Absolutely none. Remember that a small percentage out of a small number is a great deal better than a zero percentage out of nothing.

If you are afraid of rejection, which most of us are, you need to put this phobia aside. Most of us usually allow fears such as this one restrict us from advancing in a lot of ways, particularly socially. The thing you must remember is that no progress can occur without taking positive action.

You have to simply reduce your fear to what it really is—something your mind has created to protect you from embarrassment and hurt. You can't allow yourself to be hurt or embarrassed if you smile at someone and nod, and they do not respond back to you. Maybe they had other things on their minds at the time and they didn't feel social. Or possibly their minds were in a different place than where the both of you were.

Regardless of whatever the reason may be, you must be positive and take on the attitude of not having anything to lose. Only good can from a situation like this, and you should act on one as soon as you get the chance.

If a woman responds back with a friendly "Hello" of her own, it's quite possible that you can initiate a conversation and allow the situation to take off from there. Ask her what the best way to make something is, and find out what the best ingredients are. Or ask her if she likes a certain brand of food. Just keep the conversation going, and you might be able to get a date out of it. You just never know!

None of this is possible unless you "go for it" to some extent and make a move. If you get the cold shoulder from a woman, just move on. You are only trying to be friendly and obviously she isn't. You can't dwell on it because there are ample opportunities like these everywhere. You just have to be alert and you have to keep smiling. You really have no idea who you'll meet.

THE BEST
PLACES
TO MEET 'EM

THE BEST PLACES
TO MEET 'EM

The best places to meet women are really everywhere outside your door. Here's a quick list:

(1)   Anywhere that there is a line (post office, retail stores, ticket agencies)

(2)   Gyms

(3)   Where you live (apartment complexes, pools, gyms within complexes)

(4)   Workplace (if allowed)

(5)   Supermarkets

(6)   Bookstores

(7)   Ball games

(8)   Any type of club where you share a common interest with others (wind surfing, skydiving)

(9)   Freeways (why not?)

(10)   Laundromats

(11)   Public transit (trains, buses, subways, ferries, planes)

(12)   Department stores

(13)   Concerts, plays

(14)   Coffee shops

(15)   Restaurants

(16)   Bike riding

(17)   Running, walking, hiking

(18)   Parks

(19)   Movies

(20)   Bars, nightclubs

The list really does go on and on, but you must be aware of the fact that anywhere you go, there is the potential to meet someone.

Many women complain that they have a problem finding men. It's kind of scary for them, actually, because there are more women than men in America. Couple this with the fact that there is a growing gay community, and the list of available straight men grows smaller every day. This fact alone should fire you up considerably.

Women are looking and waiting to meet someone who is bright and unique like yourself. With this in mind, you must always look for the opportunity to meet a woman. The key here is to not "look" as though you are looking for someone. Just like when they are in a bar, women also have radar that can detect someone who is lonely and looking for someone.

You have to be casual, yet aggressive. However, if a woman gives off the signal, in so many words or actions, that she is not interested...leave her alone. If you see her responding in a friendly way, such as adding to the conversation...keep trying your best to keep it going. You never want to make her feel nervous or threatened—this is surely the quickest way to end a conversation.

How do you go about approaching a woman in an unthreatening manner? Here are some examples.

(a)   If you are in a line, say for tickets, and you spot an attractive woman without a ring on her finger, try to catch her eye. If you manage to catch her gaze, smile in a friendly way- not in a way that looks as if you are a Cheshire cat, but in a way that is relaxed and friendly.
If she smiles back and you can see that she doesn't look threatened by you, try asking her about what type of tickets she's buying. "What are you going to see?" you might ask. If she responds with a similar type of ticket that you are buying, go a step further. "Really, I am too...What night are you going?", you could say.
If she names some off-the-wall group you have never heard of before, ask her something about the group. "I've never heard of them before...What type of music is that?"
Next, if she still seems interested after whatever type of initiation you have chosen, ask her about the last concert she had attended, or what type of other music she likes. If you have or haven't heard of what she discusses, suggest casually that the two of you should go and see one of the groups she had named off. Act interested and enthusiastic. If she responds with a "maybe" or a "yes" find out where you can contact her. (refer to the chapter called 'getting the number') If she says no, then move on.

(b)   This same, basic situation can apply to wherever you happen to be. If you are at a ball game, remember where you are and ask an attractive

female what team she likes. Or you can ask her how
often she goes out to the ballpark.

(c)   If you are bike riding, ask her how her ride is going,
or how she likes the area. Just like in the other
examples, the environment provides easy topics to
initiate conversations with, so use it.

I have always believed in trying to catch a woman's
eyes before speaking with her (see chapter on 'Being alert
and friendly') because I didn't ever want to startle her, or
come off seeming obnoxious. You should do the same.
Gauge the environment and what type of topics are
pertinent and be aware of you surroundings.
You need to be daring, or opportunities will pass you
by in the dozens. Take advantage of situations like these,
wherever you may be, and you'll be happily surprised at
what happens.

CONVERSATIONAL
SKILLS

CONVERSATIONAL SKILLS

This is one area where many potential relationships are blown by most men. You have to proceed with a great deal of tact and direct the conversation towards her and her interests. How do you do this?

For starters, you never, ever want to open a conversation by commenting on a woman's "big three'. This triad includes a female's most noticeable physical attributes- breasts, legs, and/or buttocks. Hopefully this doesn't come as a surprise to you, but to many males, this is very hard to believe. "What's wrong with complimenting a woman if she's got a great pair of knockers?", I have heard a lot of guys say. What's wrong is that this shows a total lack of respect on your part towards a woman. Many women already think that men only have one thing on their minds, and comments like these only confirm their beliefs.

No woman is going to get turned on by hearing how large her breasts are, especially if you say it with a half-crooked smile on your face and a beer in your hand. I recommend that you never even mention anything about her physically when you first meet her, unless you compliment her eyes. Even with eyes, you might seem a bit too forward and make her nervous, so proceed with caution.

On the other hand, smart and unthreatening compliments are great for initiating a conversation. What does this mean? An example would be complimenting a woman's outfit. This is an easy, simple way to begin. "Your blouse is really sharp...in fact so is the whole outfit.", is a basic compliment. "Those colors match your skin tone perfectly.", is another example. You can make comments about how fashionable the cut of an outfit is, such as, "Wow, where do you shop? Your clothes are fantastic." These all might sound too basic or phony, but genuine sincerity must accompany these compliments. Look, really look, at the article of clothing you are commenting on, and your compliment will seem more genuine.

Generally, women are pretty gracious about accepting these types of compliments. In fact, they are usually flattered if you seem as though you mean what you say. After all, most women, though they don't like to admit it, spend a large amount of time preparing themselves before they go out. They pay much more attention to their appearance than most men. When you point out the fact that they look especially pretty or sharp, they stand out, in a good way.

Another type of compliment that you can use to get a conversation rolling is one about a woman's nails. If the woman you want to talk to has well-manicured hands and nails, say so. But, say so casually. Remember, all compliments should be made casually, not as though they are being used as pick-up lines. Rather, you want these compliments to come off as though you really noticed something amazing on a particular female and you had to tell her about it. "You have beautiful nails...do you do them yourself?", is another compliment that can be utilized.

In addition to nails, hair can also be used as a complimentary topic. "You have gorgeous hair...It must have taken forever to fix it like that." This compliment is also positive and unthreatening, and a great lead-in to a conversation.

Keep in mind that none of these compliments are even the slightest bit threatening. This is what this whole area centers around. Your attitude must be one of "casualness", and these comments should never be insulting or obnoxious.

Once the proverbial "ice" is broken, there are certain things to remember. Never use profanity and always try to keep the conversation coming out of her mouth. In other words, try to not talk about yourself as much as you normally would want to. People love to talk about themselves. If you keep the conversation rolling by having her carry the majority of it, it will seem like a great one when it's over. She'll be in a fairly decent frame of mind and you'll be set to acquire her phone number.

How do you do this? Easily. Just continue to ask her questions about her interests, and listen carefully. Pay attention to what she is saying and don't be a passive listener and say a lot of "mm hm's". Interject into the conversation brief statements, but keep it flowing. You need to watch a woman's facial expressions and see whether or not she is passionate about whatever topic she's discussing. If she acts really animated, keep up with her excitement and act animated as well.

Listening is underestimated when it comes to establishing relationships, especially with females, so it is important to give this area a lot of attention. Recalling a fact from an earlier part of the conversation will seem impressive. So try and do this a couple of times later in the discussion. You'll seem interested and also bright enough to recount something that she had said early on, and this will score points for you.

A problem that many people discover when they first meet someone is that they become nervous and their minds go blank. They don't know what to talk about, and they shortly blow the conversation. There really are numerous topics to discuss, and you should keep a few in your head, ready to be talked about at any time. What are some of them?

I have always geared my conversations toward subjects that are mutually enjoyed and ones that can lead into dates. A good example of one of these is food. Most women love food as well as men, and it is a very easy topic to discuss since we all share a universal passion for it.

New restaurants are constantly springing up everywhere, so you can always ask what type of food is the woman's favorite and then find out where she goes to get it. You can find out if she's ever been to a certain restaurant, or if she's tried a certain dish at a certain place. If she mentions a place that she hasn't been to, or visa-versa, you can casually suggest meeting there sometime. Here's an example of a typical conversation you can have;

YOU: "It's a great restaurant...Have you ever been there?"

HER: "No, actually I haven't."

YOU: "Hey, we should go there sometime...The food is fantastic."

If she then replies, "Yes...I'd love to go", or "Maybe", then keep the conversation flowing into the next topic and note what she says. If, however, she's giving off a negative signal such as looking away from you or if she seems uninterested, try another topic or move on.

If you got a fairly positive "Yes" or "Maybe", bring up the subject again towards the end of the conversation. The key is to rehash the subject as more of a statement than a question. For example, instead of asking, "Would you like to go to dinner at so and so's restaurant with me?", you should cut to the chase. Directly, yet coolly, ask, "So, when do you want to go to so and so's to eat?". This way you sound strong and confident, yet not too pushy. The first example makes you sound nerdy and the way the question is posed might give the woman second thoughts about doing anything with you. By using the second example, the woman still has the option to back off if she wants, and she shouldn't be too threatened.

If you are getting positive vibes throughout the

conversation, such as a lot of smiling from her, or a lot of laughter, ask her to dinner. Remember that dinner suggests more of a romantic type of date. Lunch, however, is less intimate and less threatening. This maybe the way you want to go. Or, you can let her decide. "Which is more convenient for you...Lunch or dinner?". Once again, she has a sense of being in control and should not be threatened.

Cooking is another topic of discussion that can easily lead into a date. Along with dancing, women love men who can cook. I too was once a bachelor who was happy eating stew out of a can, but I quickly learned how to cook once I found out what a turn on it was to women. I also learned that it wasn't so much the taste that impressed women, but rather the idea that I was making the effort to prepare them a meal.

The moral behind all of this is "learn how to cook". When the opportunity arises , bring into the conversation the fact that you love to cook and would be willing to cook for her anytime. You will not only seem to be quite a gentleman, but also you'll appear to be strong and secure enough with your masculinity to perform domestic tasks. Many men refuse to do things such as cooking and cleaning, and this is why you should. You can still eat your stew out of a can whenever you want, but make the effort for an attractive woman. The end result will be worth it in the long run.

Many men do not make this type of effort and seem "the same as most guys" to most women. You want to be different because you'll be that much more attractive than some guy who won't cook.

Simple creativity and innovation on your part will not only make you more attractive, but allow you to grow as an individual. The more you practice cooking for women, the smoother you'll become. Then, when you really want to impress a female, you'll be more confident and comfortable with the logistics behind cooking an intimate meal.

Cooking is both innovative and creative, and let's not forget impressive. It's also usually a lot cheaper than going out to eat.

Lastly, you need to keep in mind that cooking is one area that most men overlook. They think that by taking a woman to a fancy restaurant and unloading a few hefty bucks, she will be impressed. It does impress some, but on the whole, most women tend to like the home-cooked version better.

FINDING OUT ABOUT THE "BOYFRIEND"

FINDING OUT ABOUT THE "BOYFRIEND"

Many men are very intimidated by attractive women, and the root of the problem here is the fear of rejection. The general thought is, "She's beautiful...you know she has a boyfriend". You are counting yourself out even before anything has happened Unfortunately, most men share this type of belief.

On the contrary, many beautiful women do not date very much. Why? Usually because there aren't many men with enough nerve to approach them. If they do approach them, men never seem to have enough confidence to ask them for a date.

Sure, a lot of beautiful women have boyfriends-but the key here is to subtly find out whether these women do or do not.

Firstly, you need to get over the stigma that a beautiful woman is unapproachable. Next, once you are involved in a conversation with one, you need to casually discover facts about the boyfriend situation. How? Well, you never want to ask initially, "Do you have a boyfriend?" This is much too stiff and too nerdy. You need to act as if you are unaffected by anything she says regarding a boyfriend, so you can't seem too eager.

An easy way to find out is to point out a particular piece of jewelry or clothing and then make a comment. For example, "I like that ring...did your boyfriend give that to you?". After a question like this, there are many different responses that can occur. Remember that regardless of what she says, you will find out a lot by watching and listening to her response.

There is one general type of response that we are shooting for. "No...actually, I don't have a boyfriend." Bingo! This opens up the whole situation with great possibilities from here on out.

Then there are the more ambiguous answers.

"No...actually I bought it for myself", or "No...actually my mother bought it for me".

Whatever the response may be, you need to assume a certain attitude. The assumption here is that unless she mentions her boyfriend in the conversation or she has a ring on her finger, she is probably not too serious about the guy or guys that she's dating. You need to believe that you have a legitimate shot at dating this woman.

You also need to acquire the ability to "play it off". This means that whatever she says to you, you always need to remain on an even keel. Responses by you such as, "You have a boyfriend?! Aw man, that totally sucks...I can't believe it", will never get you anywhere. If she says something about a guy she is dating, come back with a cool, confident reply of your own. "Really?...sounds pretty serious to me", you could say in a joking manner. Then she might come back with, "No...not at all...we're just friends." Then you are right back in the game.

The key is to always come back with quick and casual responses. You can't let anything she says get you down. If you do, you'll be back to square one, which is not where you want to be!

GETTING
THE
NUMBER

GETTING THE NUMBER

I have always been a firm believer in trying to meet as many women as possible, especially ones to whom I am strongly attracted. Many times, I have met them in strange and different situations, ones where I could not engage in a full-blown discussion about restaurants, politics, etc.

With this being the case, I have always tried to acquire an attractive woman's phone number very shortly after meeting her. This way you can prepare for your phone conversation and call when you are relaxed and full of enthusiasm. You can find out whether or not you like a woman over the phone, and then proceed from there.

My motto has always been, "A maybe is better than a no", and generally, if you acquire a phone number from a woman, you're at least at the "maybe" stage for asking her out on a date.

What is so great about this situation is that if after a few minutes you discover that you really don't like this person, you can say "Good-bye" and never have to talk to her again. If you take someone out and you don't really like her, you have to stick out the date and probably pay for it. This is both a waste of time and money.

"What is the best way to get a phone number?", you might ask.

Well, you never want to ask for it in a dorky way such as, "Can I have your phone number?". This is threatening as well. However, if you were to say, "Is there somewhere I can reach you?", you would sound disarming and allow her to be in control. Let her call the shots, by your insistence. All you want to do is establish some line of communication for the future when you could possibly ask her out.

Why do I believe in meeting and acquiring as many numbers from as many attractive females as possible? The main reason for this is so that there are options. If a conversation doesn't go very well with one person, go to the next. If you set yourself up in the mind-set of, "God I hope this works out.", you're in for some big letdowns.

The more women you talk to, the more you'll become comfortable with anyone. This way, when the perfect woman in your eyes comes along, you'll be ready.

It isn't that big of a deal, really. It is just a phone number, and men and women exchange them all of the time. If you're aggressive enough, you'll basically be able to write your own social calendar, with women filling the squares.

THE FIRST
DATE
AND GOING
SLOW

THE FIRST DATE
AND GOING SLOW

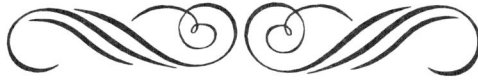

Certainly most people enjoy sex, but there are still many hang-ups concerning the act and the intricacies revolving around it. First date sex happens all of the time-but most women, in retrospect, regret doing it on the first date.

Obviously, when two people are attracted to each other, there is a great amount of sexual tension that arises. Most men want to go for the quick "kill" and worry about the woman's feelings later. This is definitely not the way to start off a successful relationship with a woman in the 90's.

We're supposed to be careful...this meaning taking precautions such as condoms and other forms of birth control, and I recommend this without any doubts. But this doesn't mean that since we have access to protection we should try and do it whenever we feel like it. What this does mean is that both a woman's and a man's feelings are involved when it comes to the inaugural toss in the hay.

By waiting until the second or third date, or "whenever it feels right" is the best way to go. Not only will the sexual tension build to incredible heights, but also the woman involved will respect you, and consequently want you, much more.

Waiting stimulates us mentally, therefore allowing us to create all types of fantasies and scenarios in our minds.

I once slept with a woman who I was good friends with. She kept saying that if we slept together, it wouldn't change our relationship at all, and that it probably would enhance it. Well, after we had gone through with it (which really wasn't the best experience in itself), I could see that something in her eyes had changed. I knew that we were going to have a lot to discuss.

She said to me the next morning that I was being "such a typical male", and she thought that it was unbelievable that I still felt the same about her and our relationship. I thought that this is what we had agreed upon. "When you enter a woman's body, emotions and feelings come into play...you just can't do it and forget about it", she explained to me. I tried to explain to her that after we had discussed it the previous night, we both had agreed to just "stay friends" and have sex just for pure physical enjoyment.

The gist of the next few statements she made were basically summed up in one statement. "Maybe you can be callous to all of the feelings involved—but women can't...regardless of what I said, mentally I have changed in regards to our relationship. I look at you differently now." The result of this was hours of arguments and discussions. "Can it be this complicated?", I asked myself. It sure can, and you really need to think about all of the ramifications involved before you actually go through with anything sexual.

I eventually found out that going slow was ultimately the best way because it allows the both of you to under-stand the situation better. Also, if you wait much longer than normal to make a move on someone, you start the woman's mind thinking about things as well. "Why didn't he kiss me? ...didn't he find me sexy? ...am I being too cold towards him?", are all questions that possibly pop into the heads of women when you play a potentially sexual situation coolly.

I believe that it's a bit unrealistic to wait for a set, certain amount of time, such as the sixth date, three months, what have you, before really trying to push the sexual issue. There isn't a standard amount of time to "get to know someone" before sleeping with them. Complicating matters further, if you purposely drag things out too long, the risk is that the spontaneity will be extinguished. Many times, if you wait too long to make a move, the woman will start feeling that you are more of a friend than a potential "boyfriend". This has happened many times with many of my close friends as well as myself, and it can really hurt your self-esteem. So when is the right time? You have to gauge this for yourself because everyone is different.

Sleeping with someone on the first date complicates matters greatly. I'm sure that there are some examples where people have slept with each other the night of their first date and the sex was absolutely incredible. But on the whole, I doubt whether this really happens enough to justify attempting it every time. The best sex, to me, comes after you have been with a partner for a while and you get to know each other's needs, likes, and more importantly, dislikes. Communication is the key to all of this.

Sex really shouldn't be filled with hang-ups and embarrassment. Rather, it should be a unique, unbelievable mental and physical ride into ecstasy. Why do women say "No" on the first date? It's not because they don't want to experience a great thing, but because of a number of reasons.

Environment has a big role here, as well as religious upbringing. Just as boys are told to be macho, girls are told to keep boys away.

Women also do not want to seem like "whores" who sleep with anyone on the first date. Typically, it is believed that a woman is a "whore" if she allows a man to have intercourse with her on the first date. On the other hand, a man "scores" if he gets laid in the initial outing. This is a double-standard no doubt, but stigmas such as these help perpetuate many of the hang-ups concerning our sexual behavior.

It's tough sometimes when your body is telling you to

"go for it" and your mind is telling you the opposite. What can you do? Well, you can try and relax and think about the consequences.

Don't you think that women are as sexually aroused as much as men are? Of course they are—but they're generally stronger when it comes to saying "no". The aforementioned examples confirm some of the reasoning behind why they say "no" and you should attempt to understand this.

Another example of this reasoning is also a strong one. Many women know that they want to sleep with a guy, but if they do, they think they'll lose him. They feel that he'll lose interest because she was too easy. You have to think about this possibility as well.

No one is asking you to be a therapist. But what you can be is someone who takes things in stride, and one who tries to understand a woman the best way you know how. Never force an issue, and remember that many feelings are involved here. If you do wait, you will be more of a gentleman and much stronger than the woman originally thought. Try and make her want you...as much as you want her.

WHEN
SHE SAYS
"NO"

♥

WHEN SHE SAYS "NO"

What really does a woman mean when she says "No"? Simply put, it means no! It also means for you to stop whatever you are doing to or with her.

Men's thinking is really screwed up in many ways when it comes to interpreting what women mean by what they say. The games played by all have led us to believe that sometimes, when a woman says "No" she really means "Yes".

You must always stop when you hear "No". If you push a situation after she says this, you will be putting the two of you in a very uncomfortable position. Many rapes occur because of the "No really means Yes" theory, and you need to always have control over yourself.

I have been with women who have openly admitted that when they have said "No" they really meant they opposite. But men are not mind readers in this respect, and women can't expect us to be so. We can only go with what we hear and feel. Women who have meant "Yes" while saying the opposite have created a vicious cycle of thinking, and this cycle needs to be stopped.

You must always interpret "No" as meaning "No" and that is that. Maybe it is a turn-on to the both of you to practice this type of behavior, but you shouldn't play any games until you know the person better. If it turns her on to say "No", let her keep saying it all she wants until she says "Yes". Up until that point, play it safe and refrain from pushing any further. This is the smartest way to deal with any female you meet.

FLOWERS
AND OTHER
GESTURES

FLOWERS AND OTHER GESTURES

On a first date, whether it be lunch or dinner, I have found that women do not receive flowers as much as they would like. By bringing flowers, it shows that not only do you like the person you are bringing them for, but also that you are caring and sensitive. "He was thinking of me when he bought these flowers...he seems really nice," is a common thought many women have after receiving flowers from a man on a first outing.

There is no woman I have ever met who does not like flowers, so you should bring them. They are generally a very inexpensive way to show your appreciation for a beautiful woman, and a nice gesture of romanticism as well.

Most men do not remember to bring flowers, so this should be another encouraging reason why you should. Never be like all of the rest.

After the first date, I believe that it is always a classy move to call the woman the next day and thank her for going out with you. If it wasn't a great date and you realize that you weren't attracted to the woman as you originally thought you were—you don't have to call. But if you had a pretty good time, and you would like to see her again, call and say "Hello".

Many men and women think, "Why should a guy call a woman after their first date and thank her?...What is he thanking her for? ...Isn't that overdoing it a bit?" The reason I suggest this is because it shows (and surprises) that you appreciated her and her company. Forget about the logistics of who paid for the date's festivities. Just make it subtly clear that you appreciate her, and you'll generally be put in good standing.

Many women complain that generally after the first date, or the first time they meet a guy, he waits forever, if ever, to call. The theory for guys here is to "make her wait a bit. Let her think about me." The result is that women eventually get fed up with waiting for the call and go on with the other guys.

My feeling here has always been to call the woman the next day briefly, and then proceed from there. Perhaps you can set up another date for later in the week or what have you. If you do set something up, wait a while (whether a matter of two to three days) and then call again to confirm your plans. If you call every day right in the beginning, you could sound a bit too eager and/or desperate.

Waiting two to three days between calls allows the woman to think about you a bit- but remember, you don't want her forgetting about you or losing interest. This could happen if you wait a week to two weeks before making the call. Everyone has some insecurity, and if you don't call this person for quite a while, they are going to think that you didn't like them very much. Don't resort to head games like these so that you can gain the "upper hand" over the woman. Most women won't tolerate those types of games these days, so don't play them.

The truth of the matter is, if a woman is fairly attractive, you can assume that she probably has other guys calling her—not just you. Your chances of competing with these guys get smaller and smaller when you don't act smart.

Another important facet to phone etiquette is to always call when you say you are going to call. If you tell a woman that you will call her tomorrow, call her tomorrow! Nothing is more frustrating than waiting for a phone call and not receiving it.

If you tell a person that you are going to call them at

a certain time on a certain day, and you don't—it is pretty insulting on your part. Reverse the roles and think about what it is like when a woman promises to call you and she doesn't. You might start thinking that maybe she felt you were boring, or obnoxious, or whatever else your mind can conjure up.

There are always some exceptions- emergencies for example. But try to avoid situations like these from happening, especially in the beginning stages of a relationship. Always make a conscious effort to follow up your words with action. Women respect men who fulfill their promises and are not just "all talk".

Flowers and phone calls are just two ways that make you more desirable to desirable women. They take virtually no large amounts of time, and anyone can perform them. Don't sit on your pants and blow something good when you see it. Make efforts like these...always.

MEN'S ROLES IN TODAY'S SOCIETY

MEN'S ROLES IN TODAY'S SOCIETY

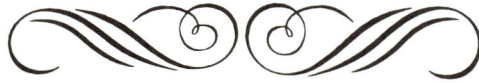

　　The women's lib movement of the 1970's and 1980's brought about many important issues that needed to be addressed concerning women's treatment in today's society. This brings us to where we are now, in the 1990's, and the ideas of ever-changing men's roles. Men have become increasingly confused about their roles and how they are "supposed to act" in regards to the opposite sex.

　　Women today are most definitely perceived as stronger and more capable than in previous decades such as the 1950's, where they were only supposed to be housewives. They were expected to stay home, cook, clean, and take care of the kids. Meanwhile, men were supposed to stay out and bring home the bacon because they were the only breadwinners of the household.

　　These times are unlike any in the past. Two-income households are almost a necessity if a family is to progress both economically and socially. Traditional values have been twisted somewhat, thus leaving many men shaking their heads, confused.

　　Though I believe I am a traditionalist when it comes to dating, I have been caught off-guard by some women who have made me feel a bit "out of touch" initially in a relationship.

　　For example, I believe that a woman should always be treated like a lady. To me, this means helping her off curbs, holding open doors for her, and the like. I have been on quite a few dates where, when I attempted to help my date off of a curb, she has responded almost angrily. "I'm not so lame that I can't walk by myself," or "Believe it or not,

I am actually strong enough to open my own doors, thank you!" are two typical responses I have heard.

At first, my eyes widened a bit and I joked along with them, trying to make it clear than I wasn't patronizing them, but rather that I was old-fashioned. I went further in saying that I believed that a woman should always be treated like a lady. These gestures, I explained, were my way of showing my respect. After this, tensions eased considerably.

Virtually all, after this point, enjoyed how I treated them, once they understood my reasoning behind my behavior.

A women is taught that she should be able to stand on her own two feet, and this, to me, is great. I love women who are strong, and there are many of them out there. I still believe, due my own personal experience, that they still want to be treated like ladies in old-fashioned terms.

The whole point of this is the concept of respect. Women, as well as men, want to be respected, and they should be. I always open doors for women, but I also feel out the situation. If they come off as strong as opposed to meek and in need of care, I'll sometimes ask them if they mind me doing certain gestures. Many, if not most, like to be treated this way, and willingly accept this type of treatment. Try not to ever make a woman feel weak, or you'll quite possibly receive the same reactions that I did. Those situations called for some quick thinking, and luckily, my honesty paid off.

"What about paying for the first date?" With roles today being what they are, many women offer to pay for dates, especially first ones. I have always felt that if you ask someone out on a date, you should pay for it. I am not advocating that you should go into debt, but I feel that it shows an acceptance of responsibility and a caring on your part if you pick up the tab.

If a woman absolutely insists that she pays, try to make an agreement where she can pay for the second date. Explain to her that since you asked her out, you want to pay. Besides, if you really like the woman, you can get some reaction from her after you suggest a second date. Watch her reactions, they'll tell you more than you think.

SENSE
OF
HUMOR

SENSE OF HUMOR

When surveyed, a great majority of women always select a "sense of humor" as being the number one reason for being attracted to someone.

Everyone has a sense of humor, however, some choose to display it more than others in many different ways.

It's great to be around someone who is good-natured and has a funny perspective of things. Self-mockery is a great way to allow one's humor to come out, in a non-threatening way. How is this done? Say, for example, you are very thin. You can mock yourself by saying something about how big your muscles are, or aren't. Or you can talk about things that are the most embarrassing to you, and situations that you have been in that are embarrassing. If you are blatantly honest, stories like these are usually hilarious. Remember what works and what doesn't, and use similar anecdotes and stories for other conversations as well. If you make fun of yourself you are perceived as a secure individual. Insecurity comes out a lot when someone is constantly ripping other people behind their backs.

You should never push your humor on anyone. You have to use your best judgment If, in a conversation, a situation arises where you can joke about it, give it a shot.

But try not to be obnoxious. Some guys just will not give up. Remember that if something is funny to you and no one else, keep it to yourself. Maybe try a different approach, but don't get discouraged. Just look for the proper times for your humor, and you'll keep a humorous edge on your conversations, without trying to sound like a comedian.

GETTING
SEXY

GETTING SEXY

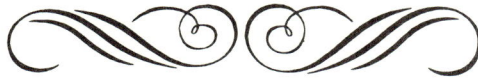

Where does sex appeal come from? It comes from within, but it also encompasses everything about you. Your attitude towards things, such as your body, and the types of clothing you wear, has a dramatic effect on what others perceive as sexy.

How do you get sexy? Look at all of the movie stars and models. Why are they so sexy to women? Generally, the reason is because they're physically beautiful and they are what they are...actors and models. This is why they get paid huge amounts of money to display their bodies all over everywhere. Their bodies are always in shape. Does this clue you in a bit more?

A sexy body is one that is a combination of muscle, definition, and the least amount of fat that is possible. Women do like the occasional teddy bear, but mostly they like a man who is in shape. If you are a person who despises exercise, it's time to change your way of thinking.

Just like with your wardrobe, taking care of your body shows that you have respect for yourself and that you are in touch with your body. This is truly a turn-on to women. It's time to get acquainted with weights if you are unfamiliar with them, and a cardiovascular program is also needed to round out your workouts.

Which parts of the body are the sexiest? Arms, legs, butts, and abdominals, not to mention chest, are all big turn-ons to women and you should focus on your entire body. A lean body is better than a fat one. The reason for this is because if a woman touches you, she doesn't want to grab a hunk of fat. Do you think this would be attractive? I don't think so. However, if she grabs your arm and feels a rock-solid piece of muscled flesh, she'll definitely remember what it felt like.

Too many people say, "Screw it...I'll work out next week." You can't have an attitude like this. You really don't need to be in the gym for three hours every single day, but you should do a little bit at least three to five times a week. Once you get into the habit of doing it, it won't be so hard to maintain. You just need to think about the benefits.

Working out not only makes us look better, it also raises our self-esteem and confidence levels. I know that after a work-out, I feel ready to take on the world and I have a bounce in my step. If I don't, I tend to feel lazy and unattractive. Which would you rather feel? Hopefully the first example.

How do you act sexy? Well, once you have your body in better shape, you can choose your clothes to accentuate your shape and your attitude. Showing off your arms or your broad shoulders is an easy way to grab attention, but mainly sexiness is in your attitude. If you just act natural, as I have pointed out in other chapters, your sex appeal will find a way to come out. A woman, after finding out more about you, can mentally see how sexy you are. You just need to push her thinking in this direction. By getting your body into a sexier condition than it is now can only help, so do it!

DANCING

DANCING

Men, especially Caucasian men, have no clue when it comes to dancing. They generally think that they look pretty good out there on the dance floor, but on the whole, most of us sorely lack coordination and skill.

On the contrary, women love to dance. I don't know where this love comes from or who instilled it within them, but this love is strongly there. Men need to band together and recognize this immediately. Why? Because it's something they love to do, so we should get better at doing it with them.

A woman likes to be with a guy who is a good dancer—or at least one who doesn't fully embarrass her on the dance floor. Remember, many women believe that they can judge a man's sexual performance by the way he dances. This sounds pretty strange, but it is true.

The key to all of this is to check yourself out in a mirror. Most of us are really surprised when we see ourselves flailing around uncontrollably. You need to remedy this problem in a hurry. Sure, this is one area that I could do without. But I have realized that it's one area that will probably never go away, so I have made myself as comfortable as possible with it.

I was once told by a dance-loving female that "It is better to not move enough than to move uncontrollably when dancing." Nothing is more embarrassing to a woman than to be on a dance floor with a guy who is totally off-beat and out of rhythm. It really is high time for the mirror.

Before going out, check out your moves in the mirror and see exactly what you look like. This way you can exercise some judgment on your actions. If you do happen to look pretty out of control—consult a woman-friend. Try to not be embarrassed. Keep in mind that this little amount of embarrassment will be worth a lot to you once you get a comfortable style of dance down pat. Most women can dance, and this is the reason to consult them, not one of your buddies.

Listen to the bass rhythm of a song when you're dancing. If you move with the bass you'll have a much easier time getting around the dance floor. Guys who stand in the middle of the floor playing air guitar generally look like idiots. They themselves don't think of this at all— and that is why they don't do very well when it comes to meeting women at a dance club.

Something else to remember is that it's a bad move to try to dance with a woman who's already dancing. Many women find this irritating. It also makes you seem "wimpy" in their eyes. You may think that it's an easy way in to meeting them—but it's not.

Just like the rest of the areas when it comes to attracting women, preparation is needed. If you prepare properly to meet someone, the whole process will go much smoother than it is now...for most of us. Little areas such as the way someone dances really are big areas in many women's eyes. This is why you need to be as polished as possible if you want to meet and attract. Dancing is definitely one area that needs to be polished, so get some help, if needed, and keep going for it.

MANNERS

MANNERS

Like hygiene, manners are pretty basic. However, most women complain that men usually do not have any. No...not you. You probably always practice good manners. Even with this being the case, manners should get extended further than just "using the right fork at the dinner table".

Manners also include chivalry. Chivalry may sound like an outdated word, but it needs to make a comeback in your life...starting now.

What do I mean by chivalry? Simply put, it means treating a woman like a lady. Many men hold the attitude that women today are strong, which they are, but they don't want to be treated with ultra-respect and courtesy. It makes a man feel feminine if he goes "overboard" to a certain extent. Wrong!

The great majority of women want and need to be treated like ladies, yet there is such a small, minute percentage of men who are willing to accommodate them. You need to make the effort, because it makes a big difference when you do. It separates you from the other unwilling, lazy men who couldn't care less about this topic. It's easy to "score points" with the opposite sex by following some easy basics.

Try to memorize and practice the following when the opportunity arises:

(1) Always open any door for a woman. (restaurants, malls, cars—all are good places to practice "getting smooth" at these techniques. This way, when it really counts, i.e. on a date, you'll seem very polished).

(2)   Always help a woman on and off of a curb. (Sounds too much? Believe me—it works)

(3)   Always allow a woman to "go first".

(4)   Always help a woman on and off with her coat.

(5)   Always help a woman up from sitting down.

(6)   Always help a woman into her chair.

And some serious nevers:

(1)   Never use profanity around a woman.

(2)   Never belch or fart around a woman.

(3)   When talking with a woman, never let your attention drift when another woman walks into the room or past you.

(4)   Never talk to a woman's breasts.

(5)   Never talk about past girlfriends. (Once you get into a relationship, you'll have plenty of time for discussing that)

These really do make a huge difference. If you practice them all of the time, the more attractive you'll be to all women—not just the ones that you want to attract. It may seem really awkward, but it's smart to make the effort. Remember, separate yourself from "all of the other guys" and you'll be remembered.

SENSITIVITY

SENSITIVITY

The nineties' man is strong and sensitive. Is this possible? You'd better believe it. The question remains, however, "How can a man both be strong and sensitive?" Well, it's not easy, but it's also not impossible.

The macho man believes that sensitive guys are wimps. Wimps cry and aren't tough...so it goes. But being sensitive has nothing to do with being "wimpy". Everyone probably has their own definition of the meaning of sensitivity, but it seems to me that it usually is a negative one.

To me, sensitivity means that a person has a decent sense of his or her feelings, i.e., what makes a person feel a certain way, good or bad, towards things. It also means that a person can express these feelings, has some compassion for others, and is not insecure with his masculinity to the point of where he covers up all of his emotions with a "tough guy" facade.

To actually be able to sit and listen to someone's problems, and feel with them during the entirety of the conversation, is a very attractive quality to most women. The fact of the matter is that it has always been important, it just has never been accepted by the general public.

In addition to this, having the ability to reverse the roles and express one's own feelings is just as important. It is quite embarrassing to most men to try and explain why they are feeling "hurt" towards something. This is the natural pattern most of us have fallen into. It is important to remember though, that it is generally better for all parties concerned to express feelings, rather than suppress them and become callused and hardened.

Women can see through shallowness, and they know when you are putting on an act. You should never have a fear of thinking that a women will think that you are weak if you don't act macho all of the time. It's one of the healthiest things you can do if you openly allow yourself the freedom of expressing your feelings. It really does help you grow as an individual.

I am not preaching that you should immediately go out and cry on someone's shoulder all of the time. But you need to maintain a healthy balance of what you should be emotional about with others, and what you can deal with on your own. Remember, women do not want to be around someone who is constantly complaining about everything. Rather, they want to be with someone who more resembles a "knight", and is strong and exciting.

Women like sensitive men...plain and simple. But they do not like wimps. Therefore, most men need to be a little less macho and a bit more sensitive. This is vital if you want to attract the quality woman of your dreams.

The saying goes, "If you cry or something bothers you, you're a sissy". This is pretty common language around many American households. It is no wonder why men have such huge problems with this area.

They have always been taught to act a certain, rigid way, and now this has all changed. It is a tough subject to deal with because a man believes he is supposed to be hard—i.e., "bring home the bacon." Now, most women want someone who is not so hard, and someone that can be more of an emotional equal with them. What do you do? For starters, you have to stay open-minded and be yourself. This does sound a bit cliché, but being yourself is ultimately the way you are going to attract whoever you want to attract. Next, you toss the "tough guy" image and begin gaining confidence in the real you. You have feelings, just like women, and you should allow them to come out whenever they need to.

Sensitivity is a big part in the role of attracting women in the nineties, and loosening up a bit will attract females beyond belief. Show your compassion, passion, and general feelings towards topics, and women will begin to be attracted to the real you, not the fake one. It sounds scary, but once you begin, the easier it will be.

STYLE

STYLE

If you are uncomfortable with some part of your body, it's time to rid yourself of these feelings. The easiest way to do this is to update your style.

Many men are basically clueless when it comes to fashion and individual style. Oh, they have their own style no doubt, but it's probably one that won't be gracing the pages of any men's fashion magazines.

The key is to always look sharp, yet feel comfortable. "What is sharp?" Well, most people generally wear what they think is most comfortable. This is fine, but if you want to attract a quality woman, wearing sharp clothes will ease the process considerably.

If you happen to be stuck in the 1970's fashion-wise, it's time to get out. Even if you wear clothes from the mid-1980's, they probably also look a bit off, or out of fashion. If you want to attract women, you must change and adapt to the changing world of fashion.

First off, you must get a general idea of what is "in". The best way is to page through men's fashion magazines and also advertisements from the larger retailers. Familiarize yourself with the colors and materials that are currently popular. For example, if it's summertime and you are in the habit of wearing heavy, plaid flannel shirts, it's time to wake up and make a change.

You must make this style change a high priority in your everyday life. I am not saying that you should go into debt purchasing new clothes every week, but there are a few basics that everyone needs to look fashionable. You need basic outfits for different times and events, and the following will help guide you through this:

(1)   A clean pair of blue jeans—Not a pair of designer jeans with extra bright stitching from 1979, but a modern pair of fashionable jeans. These can not only be worn casually, but they also can be dressed up with a blazer and sport shirt.

(2)   Dress pants—No polyester is allowed here. You need quality, pleated trousers, with a slightly baggy fit to them. They must be long enough, where they cover your socks and they must have a break at the ankle. Make sure they fit your waste properly and are neither too tight nor too loose. Colors will be determined later, with the help of a female salesperson.

(3)   Shirts—a plain, white T-shirt goes with everything. Also, you need to have a plain, white sport shirt.

(4)   Blazer—you need to have a blazer that can go with as many different combinations as possible. Black is a wise choice here. You also want a material that can go with jeans as well as slacks, crossing over, once again from casual to dressy.

(5)   Shoes and Belts—shoes are so important, yet so many men overlook this fact. They think that since shoes are way down near your feet, no one's going to notice. Wrong! You need a casual pair of dark loafers as well as a dressier pair to go with slacks. A general fashion rule is to never wear shoes that are lighter than the color of your pants. A new pair of tennis shoes is also recommended. Remember, you must find out what shoes go with which outfits. The wrong color combination can throw off an entire look, so make it a priority to understand your colors. Match your belts with your shoes. Modern leather belts in black and brown are recommended.

(6)   Underwear—immediately throw away your old, 'holey' underwear. This is about as sexy as receiving a bill in the mail. I have always been a fan of boxer shorts and today there are many different styles to choose from. Women now also find them very sexy. Purchase some comfortable, fashionable underwear. If you can't get advice on socks, stick with solids that coordinate with what you are wearing.

With all of this in mind, it's time to head down to a fashionable men's clothing store and speak with a salesperson. I recommend that you deal with a female if one is available.

The reason I recommend this is because they will tell you what looks best and what doesn't. Listen to them. You are getting free advice from the gender you are trying to attract in the first place. Of course there are some salesmen who can do just as adequate a job as women, but I have always had more confidence in a woman's opinion when it comes to fashion and color combinations.

From the beginning, you should be honest with the salesperson about your budget. However, I firmly believe that this is one area where you need quality stuff. If it means not eating out for a month or putting your purchases on a credit card, I still believe that it's worth every penny to look sharp. You only need a few basics, not an entirely new closet full of clothes. Just pick and choose wisely. You won't have to sacrifice too much to acquire something so vital in attracting women.

The only real way to learn about style is to ask loads of questions. There really aren't any stupid questions. No one is going to laugh at you for asking a "dumb" question. This is what sales associates are for- so ask away.

Ask about which colors go together, and what shoes go with what type of slacks, and when you should wear a certain type of outfit. It is important to find these things out, because you don't want to wear a great outfit at the wrong place or time.

Women notice a sharp-dressed man. If you have extra weight around the middle, tell the salesperson that you want to cover it up. If you are too thin, purchase colors and cuts that make you look heavier. Fashion is wonderful in this aspect because it really can hide most of our imperfections. Communicate with the salesperson and before long you'll have an updated wardrobe—put together especially for you.

Along with your clothes, you also need to keep your hairstyle updated. If you don't have any, or just some, you should always keep it neat, trimmed and combed.

You need to realize something about hair. Most men are going to lose theirs. You must come to terms with this now. Insecurity preys on this because we have made it such a big deal. If you talk to most women, they really don't mind whether you have some or not. Joking around about it, and making light of the situation will quickly have people forget that you have thinning hair. Let your personality take over and stop looking at the situation with fear. I have talked to many women about the subject, and they really couldn't care less, as long as the man has a sense of humor about it.

Now, if you do have some to work with, go to a stylist and tell him, or her, that you want a change. You probably don't want anything too exotic or drastic at first, but rather just an updated version of your current style.

Once again, paging through men's magazines can only help. It is important to remember that anytime that there is a change in one's personal style, especially through the recommendation from someone else, we are going to be on the defensive. Try to stay as open-minded as possible, and be willing to compromise.

It's the 90's now, and now is what we are living for, not 70's or 80's. It's time to get with it if you want to attract and meet.

Once you have a decent hairstyle, you have to

maintain it. Go back every few weeks, or whenever the hairdresser recommends, and shape it up. A decent stylist is a wise investment. I know so many who refuse to go anywhere else but to the same barber for the past twenty years. If he can't cut your hair any differently than the way he currently does, it might be time to bid him a fond farewell. You need a fashionable hairdo, not one that looks as though someone put a bowl over your head and started chopping.

A lot of times, men look at models and say that they want their hair to look like what they see in the magazines. Yet, they still refuse to use gels and sprays. These are common men's staples nowadays, and you shouldn't have any hang-ups about using them. Don't be afraid...they can only improve your look.

Once you have all of the basics that are needed, you have to get into the correct frame of mind to wear what you have.

Step one is to make sure that your clothes are always pressed and laundered. I have seen guys with great haircuts and they seem to have some style, and then I look at what they're wearing and it's dirty or wrinkled. This is very important to note. If your stuff looks slobby, you'll look like a slob as well. Take a few minutes of preparation to straighten up your outfit before going out—it'll pay off and reflect the respect you have for yourself...more than you now think.

However, if you just aren't buying into this whole "look sharp" thing, let me remind you of something. Have you ever seen a beautiful woman who dresses well, with a guy who dresses goofy? Not usually. Even if the guy isn't very physically attractive, he usually will have good clothes and a sense of style. This fact alone should be enough to make you change your thinking.

You might be saying, "Hey, what about the myth about the fact that a woman will be attracted to me, not my wallet or clothes, etc.?" Your wallet and how much you spend has nothing really to do with dressing well. Sure it will cost a few bucks to update your wardrobe, but you won't need to spend an outrageous amount of cash to purchase top designer fashions.

I like wearing jeans, mostly with T-shirts, and it's okay to feel this way. As long as you keep mixing up what you wear and you keep your things clean, pressed and fashionable, you'll have no problem.

Remember, lime-green leisure suits with white stitching are out...keep this in mind while shopping.

HYGIENE

HYGIENE

No one, and especially not a woman, likes to be around anyone who is unkempt, smells bad, or has bad breath.

Cleanliness and good personal hygiene sounds basic, but amazingly there are so many of us out there who forget little things which, unknowing to us, turn people off.

Let's start from the beginning. You should always wash your hair...at least once a day. Dandruff and overly oily hair turns anyone off.

Your face is also very important—primarily because this is where your mouth is located. Bad breath is one of the biggest turn-offs in the history of mankind. Always, always, always keep your teeth clean and free of scum and your breath fresh. Always. There is nothing worse than trying to talk to someone at close range that has just eaten a garlic and pesto pizza or something similar. You may love garlic and onions, as I do, but you need to keep yourself loaded with an arsenal of mints and breath drops. Keep mouthwash in your car because you just never know!

Body hair has a funny way of creeping up in places that we really do not notice. Keep your ears, nose, eyebrows, underarms, back and chest trimmed and neat. Some women love hair, but not the kind out of your nose that your can braid into corn rows.

Always remember to shower before going out into public, and use a good deodorant. Body odor is also an awful turn-off.

When it comes to cologne, never wear too much. Simple guidelines for this are as follows. Simply put enough touches on your body so that the only way anyone can smell it is if they get close to you—this meaning within two feet. It's really a turn-off when someone walks into a room ten feet away, and your nostrils burn from the half-bottle of cologne that was poured all over the clown. Many men put on so much because after a certain point, your sense of smell shuts down and you can't smell the cologne anymore. So the natural reaction is to want to put on more. Don't, you probably have on too much as it is.

Lastly, you should keep in mind that many men neglect their hands when going out to meet. Dirt under one's fingernails is gross, and gives off the message that you are a dirty person. Nails need to always be cleaned and cut neatly.

Sounds like a lot of work? I hardly think so, when it means attracting or not attracting someone. All of these are habits that must be practiced. Believe me, they will allow the attracting process to go along much smoother than if you don't practice them.

MY STORY

MY STORY

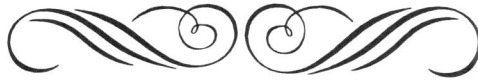

So what's my story? Well, without trying to sound like a braggadocio, I have to say that I have never had any trouble getting dates. I love women and I have always tried to be around them as much as possible. In fact, most of the time I would rather be around female companions as opposed to male ones.

I was at a point in my life where I was dating about four to five different women per week...this doesn't mean that I was sleeping with all of them, just dating. I was getting burned out, not so much physically, but rather mentally, because it seemed as if all of the women were the same. I found myself telling the same stories about myself and listening to similar ones over and over.

I usually always reserved Friday nights for my buddies. It was the only night that the five of us "hung out", usually at bars. I never went there to meet anyone, but rather to spend eight or nine hours with the four guys that were the most hilarious I had ever met. We had grown up together and it was special because we all had different careers, yet we remained very close.

Every week we would frequent the "City", or San Francisco. We had been doing this since we were eighteen, sneaking into any place that we could. One Friday night, one of the guys suggested that we head across the Golden Gate Bridge to Sausalito, which is a very popular tourist trap. The reason was because a new, hot place was opening up, and the place was supposedly going to be filled to capacity with gorgeous women.

We got to the downtown area and parked. I remarked to my closest friend that I was getting a little tired of doing the same thing, every Friday night, and maybe it was time for me to get a "serious" girlfriend. He laughed and said, "You?.. never...you love women too much to be with just one." As we walked down the main drag, which was spotted with restaurants, I happened to look over to the right just when two guys and the most beautiful, exciting creature I had ever seen were leaving.

I was completely mesmerized by her smile and presence. I couldn't believe the feelings I was immediately experiencing. Butterflies by the dozens were floating around in my stomach as I stood in one place while my friends kept walking. I had to meet her...I just had to. She looked at me and proceeded to walk by as I gently tapped her on the arm as she was passing. "You can't leave...I just got here", I said as she stopped and replied, "Excuse me?"

Her features were so startling and she was really having an effect on me. Here I was, pondering the idea of writing a book on this subject, yet I couldn't think straight. I asked her what her name was. "Alessandra", she said. "A beautiful name for a beautiful woman," I thought to myself.

The two of us instantly had a "thing" going. She was not only gorgeous, but she was also very intelligent. I stumbled through our brief conversation enough to get both her work and home phone numbers. She smiled at me and walked away, and I couldn't stop thinking about her for the rest of the evening. In fact, I didn't sleep much that night. I kept going over what I was going to say when I called her that morning. Sounds anxious to you? You had better believe it.

I called her that morning at her work and scheduled a date with her for the next day, which was a Sunday. I had to bartend that Saturday night, and there was no way out of it. I considered calling in sick...which would have been the first time I had ever done that. But, I didn't and I was in a trance the entire evening thinking about her.

I picked her up that Sunday evening and as she answered the door, I was again startled by her presence.

I felt wonderful talking to her, smelling her perfume, staring into her eyes. In other words, I had fallen head over heels in love with this woman. Everywhere we went that night I announced that she had just said "Yes" and that she was now my fiancee She thought I was a bit crazy, but I didn't care. I was crazy about her.

Keep in mind that she was dating other guys and she herself had bartended...so she knew all about that scene and the number of people that a bartender tends to meet. She was very wary of me from the beginning. I sent her flowers, wrote her poetry, called her and in a very old fashioned way, courted her. I asked her to marry me six months later and she did actually say "Yes".

As for all of the other women I had dated—I never went out with any of them after I had met Alessandra. She greatly enhances my life and is my closest confidant and friend.

The moral to all of this is that if I had not been aggressive and spurned to meet this wonderful person, I would have blown an incredible opportunity. By applying all of my techniques, I was able to meet a woman beyond my dreams of the "perfect woman". It can happen to you as well, but you need to have confidence that anything is possible. You may get shot down on occasion, but when you meet the right person, you won't be able to control the overwhelming sensations that come over you. It's worth the effort...I know because I am living a virtual dream.

AND AWAY
YOU GO

AND AWAY YOU GO

Wow! You have actually come to the ending without falling over from boredom (or sleep). The content seems to be pretty basic, huh? Well, if you believe this you are in the perfect state of mind to begin attracting women in the '90's. Obviously, if you have read from start to finish, you probably have an inkling to the way I have always attracted women. I really do hope that I haven't come off as some type of sexist pig, because I know that I am not. I just believe in my techniques and I also believe that with the proper application, they can work for anyone. If I didn't truly believe this, I wouldn't have written a book about it.

Remember that attitude plays such a huge part in your everyday interaction with women. You need to feel good about yourself first before anything else. Review the chapters and allow yourself to be open and honest. This is sometimes very difficult, but it is something that needs to be done. Every person is attractive in his or her own way, you just need to find out what way that is, and concentrate on it.

Obviously, the majority of men who have read this book want to better their ability to attract the opposite sex. You probably have as well. This is good, but none of these theories are worth anything unless you get out there and "go for it." Don't hold back and convince yourself that you'll "go for it" tomorrow. That's the lazy way. Start feeling good about yourself now and get out there. You just never know who you'll attract!

ORDER BOOKS FROM R & E AND SAVE!

TITLES	ORDER #	PRICE
The Art of Attracting Women *Find Exactly What You Want! A must for single men!*	041-2	$8.95
Marrying For Life: *The Challenge of Creating a Lasting Friendship*	039-0	$11.95
Becoming a Sexually Intimate Person *Conquer your fears and insecurities!*	042-0	$14.95
Imaginative Healing: *Using Imagery For Growth and Change*	043-9	$11.95
Death Is... Lighthearted Views of a Grave Situation *You've seen it, now share DEATH!*	965-2	$7.95
Single Again: *Dating & Meeting New Friends The Second Time Around*	878-8	9.95
The Dictionary of Love, Sex, Marriage and Romance *You'll love the thousands of great lines and definitions!*	900-8	11.95
Equal Partners: *The Art of Creative Marriage*	761-7	9.95
How To Find A Lasting Relationship *The Most Complete Guide For Singles Ever Published*	779-X	9.95

ORDER ANY 4 TITLES & GET ONE FREE—PLUS FREE POSTAGE!

Please rush me the following books. I want to save by ordering four books and receive a free book plus free postage. Orders under four books please include $3.00 shipping. CA residents add 8.25% tax.

YOUR ORDER

ORDER #	QUANTITY	UNIT PRICE	TOTAL PRICE

PAYMENT METHOD

❏ Enclosed Check or Money Order

❏ Master Card

❏ Visa

Card Expires _____

Signature _____

RUSH SHIPMENT TO:

(Please print)

Name _____

Organization _____

Address _____

City/State/Zip _____

R & E Publishers ● P.O. Box 2008 ● Saratoga, CA 95070
● (408) 866-6303 ● FAX (408) 866-0825

ORDER BOOKS FROM R & E AND SAVE!

TITLES	ORDER #	PRICE
The Art of Attracting Women *Find Exactly What You Want! A must for single men!*	041-2	$8.95
Marrying For Life: *The Challenge of Creating a Lasting Friendship*	039-0	$11.95
Becoming a Sexually Intimate Person *Conquer your fears and insecurities!*	042-0	$14.95
Imaginative Healing: *Using Imagery For Growth and Change*	043-9	$11.95
Death Is... Lighthearted Views of a Grave Situation *You've seen it, now share DEATH!*	965-2	$7.95
Single Again: *Dating & Meeting New Friends The Second Time Around*	878-8	9.95
The Dictionary of Love, Sex, Marriage and Romance *You'll love the thousands of great lines and definitions!*	900-8	11.95
Equal Partners: *The Art of Creative Marriage*	761-7	9.95
How To Find A Lasting Relationship *The Most Complete Guide For Singles Ever Published*	779-X	9.95

ORDER ANY 4 TITLES & GET ONE FREE—PLUS FREE POSTAGE!

Please rush me the following books. I want to save by ordering four books and receive a free book plus free postage. Orders under four books please include $3.00 shipping. CA residents add 8.25% tax.

YOUR ORDER

ORDER #	QUANTITY	UNIT PRICE	TOTAL PRICE

PAYMENT METHOD

❏ Enclosed Check or Money Order

❏ Master Card

❏ Visa

Card Expires _____

Signature _____

RUSH SHIPMENT TO:

(Please print)

Name _____

Organization _____

Address _____

City/State/Zip _____

R & E Publishers ● P.O. Box 2008 ● Saratoga, CA 95070
● (408) 866-6303 ● FAX (408) 866-0825